Business Ideas

*The Ultimate Guide to Creating
Innovative Business Ideas*

Brad Jones

CONTENTS

BUSINESS IDEAS

INTRODUCTION

I want to thank you and congratulate you for downloading the book, *"How to Generate Profitable Business Ideas"*.

This book contains proven steps and strategies on how to generate great business ideas. Statistics suggest that most startups don't make it through the first two years. Basing a company on the wrong idea is one of the major reasons behind this!

Great businesses are made before they are launched – at the idea stage. Entrepreneurs who inject the right time and energy into finding a massively awesome idea are effectively setting the stage for success. By learning to find, validate and implement ideas that have a high potential for success, you'll be one step ahead of everyone else when it comes to establishing a successful enterprise.

This book is all about that. Within its texts, you'll find a wealth of easy-to-follow action steps that you can use to find incredible business ideas. You'll also get an insightful view into the traits of a great idea. This way, you'll be able to use the knowledge you acquire from this book as a baseline against which you can judge any business idea. There's also an immensely helpful chapter in creative business thinking, design thinking, and idea implementation strategies.

In a nutshell, this book is everything you need to give your entrepreneurial ambitions a new leash of life.

Thanks again for downloading this book, I hope you'll enjoy it!

14 TRAITS OF BUSINESS IDEAS

All businesses start with an idea. The most successful corporations today started with an idea that brew in the mind of a certain individual. Ideas are the seeds that are sowed to grow into great entrepreneurship and business empires. If you get the idea wrong, chances are that you'll also get the business part wrong. I like to think of generating a business idea like a farmer choosing seeds to plant. If the farmer chooses the right, healthy seeds and plants them in a nutrient-rich plot, they will certainly grow well and lead to an abundant harvest. The seed, in this case, is the original business idea while the nutrient-rich plot of land can be compared to the market in which you implement your business idea. To be able to come up with great entrepreneurship ideas, you must understand the fundamental features of any business idea.

A good idea must satisfy, most of all, the characteristics to be accepted in the market. To start with, it must be able to solve an existing market problem. Understanding the characteristics of a business idea helps you get the 'right' mindset when you're thinking about starting a business.

1. **Market** – a business should have a good enough market to facilitate an extended stay. Availability of market is one of the most important factors you consider when evaluating business ideas. For a good idea, the market also accepts the idea. Business ideas are accepted in the market if they fulfill the existing needs and seal existing gaps. When generating and evaluating your list of potential business ideas, pay considerable attention to this feature!

2. **Customers' Needs** – most successful companies are based on solving an existing problem. Good business ideas provide a solution to a problem (or problems) that people face. The bigger the problem a business idea solves, the better it is. Later on in this guide, we'll look at how you can validate business ideas based

on their ability to provide a solution to existing market needs, and many other factors.

3. **Competitive Advantage** – this is an essential feature of any business idea. Often, the best business ideas are the ones that can leverage some advantage over the competition. This can be done by providing higher value to consumers, or lowering prices. There are dozens of things you can do to enhance your competitive advantage. Think about this feature when generating and evaluating business ideas.

4. **Distinctive** – some of the most famous companies today are so because they were based on a unique idea. Think about Facebook and how they changed our ability to communicate with friends and colleagues using everyday gadgets such as smartphones. Google was certainly not the first search engine in the world, but their simplicity and effectiveness made them distinct all the same. The distinction of your idea is what helps you get out of the crowd. A great business idea should be way better than any substitute product or service. In the last few decades, I have seen numerous beverages companies that have tried to take on Coca-Cola and failed, one way or the other.

5. **Innovation** – this is a key feature of business ideas. A good idea should be able to add value to existing products and services in the market. You need to enlarge your outlook and think outside the box when generating new business ideas. The important thing is to focus predominantly on the possible consumers and what they need. The idea you settle on should provide easier ways for production and distribution of products. You can always come up with new ways to enhance the efficiency and unique proposition of the business. Your ability to innovate will come in hard when trying to break the glass ceiling in a new market.

6. **Profitability** – one of the key reasons why you want to start a new business is profitability. You want to increase your income and gain financial independence. You want a better financial future for yourself and your kids. Thus, the business idea you settle on should generate profits – at least in the long run if not in the short term. A company has got to make a profit. Today, statistics suggest that over 90% of all startups fail within their first two years. Lack of profitability is one of the reasons. Why? Evaluate whether an idea will be well-placed to generate a profit after implementation.

7. **Focus** – success can only be attained when you concentrate your focus on one thing for a long time. If you keep on jumping from here to there, the chances are high that you're not going to be able to accomplish your goals. Your business idea should only focus on a product or service. Consider a niche that you're passionate about. You want to make sure that you'll have an easy time putting all your focus in it!

8. **Credibility** – a good business idea should have credibility. It should convince yourself and your family too, if possible. Remember that, more often than not, startups rely on the financial support of friends, family members, and lending institutions. Not many people will invest in your idea if they aren't convinced it'll work. Credibility often helps get you acquire the financial backing you may need somewhere along the way to make your business successful.

9. **Resources** – it'll take you just a few hundred dollars to implement some ideas, but millions of dollars to implement others. If you generate a great idea but don't have the financial resources to implement it, then it's no good for you. Think about whether you have the money to implement the idea you're interested in. Also check the availability of human resources and all the other specialized skills that you'll need to make it work.

Availability of raw materials, space and other resources should also be an important consideration.

10. **Simplicity** – there's beauty in simplicity. If you come up with a business idea that's a maze even to your close friends and family members, then it might not be good enough after all. Simple business ideas are implementable within a short period. If it's difficult right now, the chances are that you'll encounter difficulties that you won't be able to address in the future. Being simple is one of the most important features of a business idea.

11. **Difficulty of Duplication** – it's saddening how many entrepreneurs are coming up with great business ideas but still won't spend the time and energy to secure necessary legal protection. We see it every day. You come up with a great business idea, but then when you wake up the next day, someone who's richer has duplicated it altogether. There are thousands of lawsuits around the world where entrepreneurs are suing both individuals and corporations for 'stealing' their ideas. Have it in mind that people will always try to copy your business idea when they realize it's profitable. Before you get into business, make sure there are adequate laws in your country to protect against this kind of duplication. Focusing on a protection mechanism beforehand is a must-do if you want to keep and benefit from your idea.

12. **Legal Rights** – however excellent your idea is, you'll still need legal permits to implement it. Think about whether it's going to be easy or hard to get these permits in your country or jurisdiction.

13. **Employment Opportunity** – in most nations, especially in the developing world, unemployment is a significant problem. When explaining your business idea, you'll need to explain how many

job opportunities it can create. Thus, job creation is an important feature of your business idea.

14. **Government Support** – some business ideas get more business support than others. Think about whether you're looking for this kind of help when generating ideas for your next business. Find out what ideas your government gives priority. There are various forms of government support, including tax reduction or exemption, support for market access, reduced interest rate on loans, provision of technical and advisory services.

This chapter gives you a pretty good idea as to what features (traits) you should be thinking about when generating and evaluating business ideas. Scores of startups have failed because their originators failed to reflect on each of these features in detail. Don't let history repeat itself. Think about the market, simplicity, profitability and competitive advantage when considering your next line of business. Pay keen consideration to all these factors. Still, you'll need a lot more than a knowledge of these features to come up with rock-solid business ideas. Luckily for you, the next chapters in this book are meant to help you hit the nail in the head.

12 EASY WAYS TO GENERATE GREAT BUSINESS IDEAS

Generating a killer business idea is easy, but hard. Easy because you can close your eyes for 10 seconds and come up with a brilliant idea, and hard because it often takes a lot more than 'thinking'. The sure thing though is that there's always that great idea out there, waiting for you to find it. I have often talked to people who said that almost everything that could be invented had been invented. But this is not the case. The world is becoming more complex, and that means there are more problems to solve. The more problems there are to solve, the more ideas there are out there. Open yourself to an incredible world of possibilities. Be ready to find the most brilliant idea there is to find. And then start with these easy tips to create a rock-solid business idea.

1. Talk to Family

Talking to family about businesses is not something most people do. Sure, you'll go to them for help once your idea is developed, but talking to them early can be an excellent way to generate awesome business ideas. Donald Trump got his real estate business ideas by learning from his father, who was already a successful real estate developer. Whatever your experience your granny has gathered over the last couple of decades might be great fodder for your next business idea. A friendly family chat between NASA engineer Stephen Altemus and his son way back in 2009 led to the "first of its kind" spacecraft. There's no limit as to what you can gain from your family when it comes to gathering business ideas. Just talk to them and let them know that you want to start a new business and are looking for the best ideas.

2. Get a Boost from Friends

You'll be limiting your possibilities and narrowing the horizon if you just rely on yourself when generating business ideas. At some point, your creative juices will run out. If you haven't found the right idea by this time, you'll be back where you started. Talking to friends is another great way to find cool business ideas. Assuming you have about 16 friends, some of them may have great business ideas brewing up in their minds. Steve Jobs wouldn't have been able to build Apple Computer if he hadn't been friends with Steve Wozniak in the first place. Job didn't know a thing about the computers back then, but he had the mind for business ideas. His friendship with Wozniak made Apple happen. The point is that you should keep your ears open every time when you're looking for new business ideas. Make a point to talk to your buddies at work, home and elsewhere. Share one of the ideas you have come up with already. When you share an idea with people, they tend to come up with more ideas!

3. Think 'Around' Yourself

King Gillette was so fed up with the tiresome process of sharpening a straight edge razor that he founded the modern-day disposable razor industry. There are endless stories where people were so fed up with something that they started successful businesses from that. If something you do often is starting to frustrate you, chances are that it is also frustrating for others. It can be frustrating for millions of people, millions of potential customers. Take note of what those little things are and make a list, maybe you could come up with an incredible business idea out of that.

4. Keep Your Eyes Open

Potential business ideas are all around us. Take a short drive around your neighborhood or town and see all the thriving businesses people have set up. All these started out as mere ideas. What does that tell you? That's if you open your eyes and look, there's always one more idea for a successful business. If you do or experience something, and it piques your interest, try to figure out what's so special about it. Narrow your focus and zero in on the idea behind that 'interesting thing'. A Kenyan guy found it interesting to entertain local people by acting as some kind of action movie commentator. It might not sound like your ideal business idea, but he made millions out of it. Those little details that interest you or rub you the wrong way could all be ideas for the next great business venture.

5. Travel

Nothing opens your eyes more than traveling. If you're ready to set some time aside to look for great business ideas, consider booking a flight, or moving to another city or country. Leopoldo Fernandez discovered Domino's Pizza while on a trip to the US from his country Spain. Leopoldo was so fascinated with the whole fast-food 'thing' that he went back home and created TelePizza in 1986. TelePizza now registers over $260 million (in sales) and employs over 13, 000 people in 8 nations.

6. Focus on your interests

I know at least a dozen people who've taken up their hobbies and made successful businesses out of them. There are thousands of people who do this on an everyday basis across the world. If you have a deep interest in fitness, consider it a business idea pending evaluation. The best thing about generating business ideas from your interest is that when you're doing something you love, it's never considered work.

7. Find New Niches

You don't always have to reinvent the wheel. You can make a great business idea by looking at what the big players in the industry are missing. Figure out a way to fill in the gaps. There's always some loophole out there in that seemingly occupied industry that you can create a business out of.

8. Apply your Skills

We all have skills. Think about your skills and whether they can be implemented into a new area. You've probably heard of JMC Soundboard, a Swiss-based company that builds high-end loudspeakers. Jeanmichel Capt invested the speakers by using his experience building guitars. If you can apply your skills in a new area and create a business out of it then that is a great idea.

9. Make it Cheaper

Most companies often get started by offering their customers an existing product at a lower price. This is an excellent way to get a business going. Warby Parker is an eyeglasses company that was launched by four business school friends in 2010. Warby Parker sells prescription glasses that are regularly priced at around $300 for $95. Since 2010, they have grown and now have 100 employees.

10. Build Better Mousetraps

There are a lot of products out there that wouldn't meet your own high standards. Consider creating a better version or model. Jerry Greenfield and Ben Cohen felt that most popular ice cream brands weren't tasty enough for their palates, so they decided to create their premium ice-cream, which is now a nationwide bestseller (Ben & Jerry's). By just being picky eaters, these guys were able to launch a massively successful company.

11. Consult the World Wide Web

The internet is a great source for new business ideas. There are scores of successful entrepreneurs who got their business ideas primarily from an internet search. Most search engine today have a 'What's Hot' or 'What's New' section where you can check out new trends, hot new websites, and other interesting new facts. Make a point to check daily. You might come up with a concept or idea you would never have thought of before.

12. Do Some Market Research

This is one great way to find awesome business ideas. Pick a market sector and research it inside out. Think about what their characteristics are, and what they need. Evaluate existing business conditions and try to get a hint of what could be lacking. You might want to start your search by looking at market statistics and reports for that specific sector. If you give it a serious go, you just might be able to come up with something!

JAMES & CLAUDIA ALTUCHER – WRITING 10 IDEAS PER DAY TO EXERCISE THE 'IDEA MUSCLE.'

In addition to the idea generation methods you've learned so far, James & Claudia Altucher have come up with an excellent method that involves writing down ten ideas per day. They refer to it as exercising the 'ideas muscle'. James & Claudia explain that if you're able to keep to their method for 6 months you'll become an 'ideas machine' and it will change your life.

Your mind has an 'idea muscle' that finds great ideas. If you don't exercise this muscle, it'll atrophy. Here's a list of steps to make sure that your mind is your number one tool and resource when it comes to unearthing ideas for successful businesses.

Step 1 – Write a List of 10 Ideas Daily

Start by writing down a list of 10 ideas. It can be a list on anything. If you are an author, write a list of books you can write. If you're a musician, write a list of songs you can sing. Business people can write a list of 10 new business ideas they'd like to implement. Of course, when you're just getting started, it won't be easy. Maybe you'll write six ideas, and it'll start getting hard. You'll start thinking 'what else can I come up with?' This is when your brain is sweating as a result of the exercising the idea muscle. Think about it like exercising in the gym. Your muscles won't start building until you're breaking some sweat. Your metabolism doesn't get better when you run until you start sweating. That's the same thing that happens when you exercise your brain. Your brain starts sweating at around number 6. This means something is going on behind the scenes.

So you need to break through this and complete up to ten ideas, no matter how hard it feels.

Step 2 – Write down Precise Ideas

Focus on making sure that you're writing down the right thing. An idea is not just anything. If you write 'I will start an airline for outer space trips', you are way off the mark. Make it more comprehensible and detailed. Write down a paragraph that lays out as many details as you're able to put in a small space. If you want to write a book for Kindle Publishing, specify what topic you'll write on, what your original material will be, and how you'll put the text in the right format before publishing. That's what a full idea should sound like. So make sure the ideas you're writing down are meaningful.

Step 3 – Idea Sex

James's and Claudia's insight is that ideas have sex just like people do. Ideas have children too. The more ideas you have written down, the better, as these small ideas can evolve into a bigger better idea. For instance, Google was created through the ideas of search mating and what makes scientific research papers relevant. These were two separate ideas coming together, culminating into a multi-billion dollar company today. Ideas have no geographic border.

Summary

Here's a point- summary of this method:

1. Eat healthy, exercise and sleep a lot. Your body needs a lot of oxygen and blood flowing to your brain so you can come up with ideas.

2. Avoid negative people. Negative people will turn your ideas into trash. So if you want to cultivate a culture of generating great ideas, stay away from negativity.

3. As described above, make a list of EXACTLY 10 ideas daily. Keep track of all these ideas. You will be surprised how many incredible business ideas you'll have ready for implementation in a month or so.

4. Be patient. Of course, not every idea will be good, but don't criticize the ones that seem wrong at that time. With time, it'll become clear, and you'll be able to sieve through the list. Even the bad ideas might become good ones in time.

5. Research. The chances are that a many of your ideas will require research. In this case, you need to get the necessary information. Put together an appropriate reading list that will nourish your brain.

With this easy and simple routine, you'll become an idea machine. Before you know it, you'll have more ideas to implement than you can fathom.

HOW TO DEVELOP A CREATIVE PSYCHOLOGY MINDSET

Creativity is the process of having original ideas that are valuable. Creativity requires two key phases: *a) coming up with unique/original ideas, and b) taking a hard look at the initial idea to assess it's values.* As an entrepreneur, you need to cultivate a culture of creativity. This means you not only need to be able to come up with great ideas, but you should also be able to evaluate them.

Creative Thinking for Business Ideas

Deliberate Creativity is a creative thinking process that's considered rather formal. Deliberate Creativity not only helps you come up with great business ideas, but also helps you carry through with implementation. Below are some Deliberate Creativity models that you can use for your next startup.

Blue Skies Thinking

Blue Skies Thinking is a form of brainstorming whereby the thinking process imposes no limits on what can be suggested. Also, there are no preconceptions regarding what the solution can be. This thinking approach encourages people to contribute to as many ideas as they can. Only after contributions have stopped, will a process be initiated to evaluate which ideas may have potential in the commercial space. If you are a member of an investment group and are looking for great ideas, this is a great creative thinking approach to leverage.

Lateral Thinking

De Bono advanced this creative thinking approach. It's all about thinking that's not automatically obvious and helps find ideas that wouldn't otherwise be found through a traditional *step by logical step* approach. Also commonly referred to as 'thinking outside the box' as it instigates the thinker to generate new or unexpected ideas.

Six Thinking Hats

This is also an approach by De Bono. This is an ideal thinking approach for both individual thinking and group discussion. Six thinking hats each represent different style of thinking that can be used to generate ideas and narrow the focus of the group on great ideas:

- *White Hat (Neutrality)* – considers the available information. This step establishes facts based on the available data, what do we know and what do we need to find out. For instance, quantitative market data would be seen to have this hat on.

- *Red Hat (Feeling)* – this hat is based on instinctive gut reaction or more so emotional feelings. There's typically no justification. The majority of entrepreneurs still rely on their gut feeling or emotional feelings when considering business ideas.

- *Black Hat (Negative judgment)* – applies logic to identify barriers or flaws with the objective of finding a mismatch. This hat compels entrepreneurs to think about anything that could go wrong with the idea.

- *Yellow Hat (Positive judgment)* – this hat uses logic to identify benefits. Yellow hat is the exact opposite of black hat. Think about all the benefits of an idea. The focus is on the best things that could happen!

- *Green Hat (Creative thinking)* – focuses on statements of investigation and provocation. Tries to see where a thought goes. This hat encourages lateral thinking.

- ***Blue Hat (Process control)*** – process control entails thinking about thinking. It compels the thinker to evaluate ideas emanating from all the other five hats.

Cultivate a culture of thinking creatively. Combine this approach with the James & Claudia Altucher Method of Writing Down 10 Ideas Per Day to Exercise the 'Idea Muscle'. Most successful entrepreneurs are where they are today because they thought up a great idea in the first place!

Creative Thinking After the Idea

Most beginner entrepreneurs tend to think that their original idea requires the most creative thinking. But experienced entrepreneurs know that the initial idea is the easy part. The real creative challenges lie in the implementation and competitive business marketing later on. When it comes to creative thinking for commercial success, there's a balance you must achieve. Starting a business requires analytical, logical thinking. As a matter of fact, our training and education encourages logical thinking, teaching us to relate concepts logically. This in turn reduces our ability to add the creative side into the mix. Maybe this is why 'thinking outside the box' is so rare today.

The following recommendations can enhance your ability to build and nurture your creative business capabilities:

- ***Look for familiar patterns*** – due to the habits and routines you learned in school, new ideas appear to be similar to old ones. The best creative thinkers get results by putting dissimilar patterns and concepts side by side. For instance, an innovative entrepreneur may put investors and competitors together: most startups looking for funding never ask strategic partners, but rather just focus on venture capitalists.

- ***Look at things differently*** – if you change the way you look at things, the things you look at will change. Stereotyped notions often crowd imagination and block clear vision. It may help to imagine contradictory approaches, or rather, work with opposites. Many enterprises have found that raising the price of a product sometimes increase its status, which in turn appeals to more customers. This is a creative way to break the tie in a price war while at the same time increasing profitability.

- ***Think the unthinkable*** – you need to find a way to structure your imagination so you can be able to explore the extreme limits of alternatives. This allows you to think beyond typical solutions. Some businesses have replaced product lines that are already profitable. You probably have seen a startup make a takeover bid for a bigger, better-established company.

- ***Focus on intent*** – ever heard that 'intent is the fuel for creative thinking? Intention brings our awareness to facts our brain considers important. An excellent way to foster creativity is to generate an awareness of the feat you want to accomplish.

- ***Change the way you speak*** – if you change the way you speak, then you could also change the way you think. I have met a lot of entrepreneurs who focus on the negatives, of deficiencies of an idea. By making a conscious decision to think positively as an entrepreneur will bring success. Start by creating positive speaking patterns. Try to avoid words like don't, no and never in your business communication. This helps fuel positive, creative thinking in the organization.

- ***You are what you pretend to be*** – you probably know that attitudes go a long way towards influencing behavior. In the same way, behavior influences attitudes. Studies suggest that reality often conforms to beliefs, be they positive or negative. The Internet today makes it easier for you to pretend to be a bigger and more mature company. The good thing is that a successful business doesn't have to keep pretending for long.

It's clear that creative thinking is part of business, before, during and after implementation. Brainstorming, thinking outside the box, ideation, disruption – whatever you want to call it – is something that you must pursue every day in your business life. Let go of those things that tend to hold you back. Be brave and take risks, especially after that incredible first idea. You can train your imagination to think conceptually. Get into a culture of crafting and implementing creative ideas in your business.

DESIGN THINKING & PROBLEMS THAT NEED SOLVING

There is a new breed of truly innovative businesses that are solving problems that customers don't have yet, and creating a bold vision of a future that doesn't exist yet. Some of these companies are using a new thinking strategy known as design thinking. Design thinking is an approach to problem-solving that involves the use of a set of tools to make a decision in situations of high uncertainty that entrepreneurs face on an everyday basis. Design thinking takes a somewhat different approach from business schools, which usually focus on market research and data. Experimentation and real-world interactions are the two concepts that underlie design thinking. Although design thinking is taught in design schools as a product-creation process, more entrepreneurs are applying this concept to business. The most important thing about design thinking is that it unlocks a world of insight on customer needs. If you only have a vague idea that you're looking to develop into a business idea, design thinking is an excellent way to go about it.

Design thinking involves four stages. By attributing a key question to each of these phases, you can be able to leverage this approach to generate a new business or product.

What's the Opportunity?

This is the first question that you ask as part of the design-thinking sequence. It helps you understand existing solutions to the problems you're trying to solve. Get started by observing people in the context of their natural setting. For instance, if you want to make a better smartphone, try watching a group of about ten people use their existing smartphones in everyday life. Make a note what they like, what could be annoying to them and what tricks they may use to circumvent existing design problems. The answers to these questions help highlight problems that your customers aren't even aware they have.

What if?

This is the second question in the design-thinking approach. Take your list of problems/needs discovered in the previous step and then brainstorm on possible ways to address these needs. Be as thorough as possible, the point is to identify as many possible solutions. Get creative under the assumption that everything is possible. Have it in mind that the answers you're formulating aren't coming out of the sky. They are based on needs that you have already identified.

What wows?

After you have exhausted all seemingly possible solutions, you can graduate to the third stage (question). Think practically and pinpoint solutions that are best suited. This phase is all about bringing more data and structure to the design process. The idea is to narrow down to a few viable options.

What works?

This is the final step, whereby you make prototypes for the best options above and introduce them back to the same customers you studied at the very beginning. Make each prototype extremely simple, so you can watch and hear the interaction of the consumers with minimal interference.

Make observations, note the feedback and iterate. Create another cycle of simple prototype tests. By the time you introduce the product to market, you'll be more confident in its chances of success.

Problems That Need Solving

As long as people have problems, they'll always be looking for answers. People consistently want better, smarter and faster ways to handle daily tasks. Fortunately for you, there is still a lot of room available to improve existing solutions and products. The important thing is that you find those itchy problems and then provide ideal solutions for them.

Here's how to get started finding problems that need a solution.

- **Build a necessary product** – one critical mistake that entrepreneurs make is creating a nice-to-have product. Just because a product appeals to you doesn't mean that it'll make it in the market. Consumers are often overwhelmed by massive choices they have to make every day. Attention spans are getting shorter, and only a few products actually get noticed. You must do something differently and much better to make it in business today. Consumers demand more every day, and the only reason you're going to be their seller of choice is because you provide the quality solution they're looking for.

- **Solve nagging issues** – Google is what it is today because they made search better. Amazon is the largest online retailer today because they made B2C trade easier. Netflix provided on-demand media streaming. Uber is doing its best to improve on-demand taxi service. Think about what you can make better or smarter?

  What is the most nagging problem you can address? The easier it is for you to solve this issue, the better. You'll need to start addressing customers' needs if you want to capture their attention. However, if the product you make doesn't come across as necessary, you could still repurpose it to solve a major need. As long as you have identified a major problem for which you

27

can provide an ample solution, you have a potentially phenomenal business idea.

- Make it your passion – aim to solve a problem you can identify with, or one that you feel passionate about. When you choose an area that you are passionate about, work becomes less hassle and more about the fun.

Have it in mind that you need all the commitment, inspiration and perseverance you can muster to succeed as an entrepreneur. Where and if possible, start a business you're passionate about. Some of the most successful business people today aren't just passionate about what they do; they also are obsessed with solving a problem that matters to them. When you have the passion and fascination, nothing can put you down. Give priority to ideas that you are fascinated with.

Your ability to deliver and solve an individual problem is also an important consideration. If you realize there's an issue with a certain product in the market, and you really can't do anything to make it better, then you'd rather forget about it. Focus on a problem that you can actually solve, this just increases your chances of success!

7 WAYS TO VALIDATE YOUR BUSINESS IDEAS

Most people are excited when it comes to launching a new business based on an idea that they had. Before it comes to that, though, you need to make sure that you validate the idea to make sure that it has real potential to make it on the market. You can't just rely on your guts and say it's a GO. You need to figure out whether the business, products or services you have in mind can solve a real problem in the world. This is an important step that helps protect the time, effort and money you invest in a business. This chapter highlights some easy strategies that you can use to test and validate any business idea.

1. Define Success

First things first, you need to define a baseline of the success that you can use for the validation. Let's say you create a landing page and you get about 103 signups per week. Is that a good or a bad number? Does it signal potential or doom for this particular idea? If you can be able to operate a successful business at 103 subscribers per week, then you might want to see whether you can arrive at this figure during the validation process.

There are a number of factors on which you can base your success metric. Think about things like the opportunity cost of launching a new business. You also might want to factor in such things as the business KPIs and development costs. It's important that you define what success looks like before you go ahead with the following validation steps!

2. Use Smoke Tests

This is often an easy and excellent way to measure interest in any idea through a basic test. It involves running a low-budget advertising campaign on a social media network or craigslist to see how people respond. For instance, if you're looking to start a business about hiring house help online, place an ad that offers the services to clients. See whether people get in touch. You can run the ads on Facebook, Twitter, Google AdWords, Craigslist or just about any other platform. Most of these advertising programs allow you to specify your target audience based on a number of factors, including location, age, gender, etc.

You may also consider using a website such as www.launchrock.com, which helps you set up a quick 'Launching Soon' page. If a good percentage of the people who see your ads sign up, its means real interest, and could be a signal that it's time to take the next step – implementation.

3.   Find Help

When it comes to validating a business idea, you're better off with professional help. Find a mentor or industry advisor. These are people who have the experience you lack. Start by introducing yourself, and then make a connection. This way, you get a seasoned industry contact who can help you determine where the problems are, and how you can solve them. I understand you might be very confident in your idea, but don't make the mistake of underestimating expert help or advice.

4.   Build a Minimal Viable Product

Sometimes, and based on your product's business nature, creating an MVP (Minimum Viable Product) is the way to go. This helps you determine whether what you have in mind is a product that people really want to use. Consider investing some resources in building a working prototype. Once the MVP is ready, test it and expose it to your friends and colleagues. Also invite random people who match your customer persona to try it out. Take note of the feedback. It's all you need to judge whether your business idea has any potential.

If you want to invest in tech (e.g. mobile app), consider trying a crowdsourcing platform such as IndieGogo. Crowdfunding platforms make it possible for people to fund your idea just because they like or believe in it. This is also an excellent way to gauge interest. Of course, if no one is interested in your story/idea, the chances are high that you won't have enough customers upon launch to sustain a business.

5. Do a Survey

There are scores of websites that allow you to set up a free survey. SurveyMonkey.com is one. You can use these sites to collect information or feedback on your ideas. Create one and share it on your Facebook page, Twitter account, and elsewhere. You may also want to send it out to friends, colleagues or trusted professionals via email.

6. Assess Yourself

This might sound like a basic method, but it's certainly worthwhile. Rather than focusing on creating products that are simply 'cool', ask yourself whether you'd use this product. Put yourself in the shoes of the customer, with the same needs. If you wouldn't be itching to use this product to solve a need/problem, then it might not be a great idea after all. Before you ask everyone else, survey yourself first. Your honest input will be paramount.

7. Lastly…Trust your Gut

After you've used all the methods highlighted above, you still want to trust your gut. Maybe the idea will work, or maybe it won't. Now that you have done everything else to validate your idea, listen to what that little inner voice is saying to you.

Testing and validating your business idea is important. Again, over 90% of startups fail within their first two years. This is one of the major reasons why. Before you invest your hard-saved money into a business idea, do everything you can to make sure that the venture will end up successful. Test and test, validate. If you're convinced that people are receptive to your idea or product, be brave and take the next step.

10 STEPS FROM IDEAS TO IMPLEMENTATION

However many great ideas you have come up with so far, it won't matter if you don't implement them. Many people come up with seemingly great ideas, but fail to apply them for one reason or the other. Implementation is what separates successful entrepreneurs from mere dreamers. You are going to need an action plan, and resources, to implement your ideas. This chapter highlights a series of steps you can take to make your best ideas a business reality!

1. Identify Your Market

You did a lot of market-research work when looking for or validating your idea. You know your target market and what they need. But you still need to increase your market knowledge, especially at this stage. Is this a new or mature market? How big is this market? Try going to an industry association to get the information you need. A few hours of online research might also suffice. You need to know the numbers. Trade shows and exhibitions also happen to be a great way to get acquainted with some possible prospects and perhaps the competition. You'll want to see who's attending these industry events? Are they the prospect you are looking for? Study your competition and learn what they are selling. Try to see whether you can beat the current market price. Do you want to sell at the same price or do you wish to offer a lower price? Is the market sales cycle short or long?

Answering these questions gives you a significant startup advantage. It also helps you reduce the knowledge difference between your new firm and competitors who've been in the market for years. This also verifies whether or not your initial assumptions about the market are correct.

2.   Identify Your Customers

One of the best ways to start a business is by identifying your ideal client. Consider creating a list of questions that will help you identify the perfect client persona. This list should include questions such as:

- Is the perfect target male or female?

- Are they married?

- Do they have kids?

- How many kids?

- What motivates them to buy a particular product or service?

- How old are they?

All this is imperative because the knowledge you gather gives you an insightful view of how your own sales process should be planned. You also collect a lot of information that you can use to fine tune your product for the consumer. For instance, if you are looking to start an e-commerce business, you may find out that people want faster delivery than what is currently available in the market. Given that, you may be able to enhance your delivery schedule so that you meet this unmet demand.

3.   Start Moving and Launch

You don't always need to have everything figured out to launch your product. Sometimes, it'll be impossible to have all the questions answered before you hit the market. You should expect that hypothetical and irrational concerns will get in the way. It's okay to experiment with the core concept while still getting more input data to build your business. The important thing is that you should have mastered confidence in the idea itself.

4. Think Profitability First

Profitability is one of the primary reasons why you want to start this business. New ventures should begin by driving towards profitability. Obviously, you did a lot to validate your idea, but you'll still want to ascertain that your business can be profitable. Think about what's the quickest way to profitability. The aim is to make your startup profitable within its first three months. But this time-frame may vary, depending on the nature of your business or industry. Christensen, a serial entrepreneur who founded or co-founded 32 small business ventures, recommends that you dedicate 65% of your capital towards the drive to profitability. 25% should go towards resources (including staff) and the remaining 10% towards scaling the business. Christensen invested between five to 10 thousand dollars in his startups. 11 failed while 13 others turned into million-dollar success stories.

5. Make Failure Efficient

If you do not manage to achieve profitability within the stipulated time-frame (often three months for small businesses), the idea could still be a failure. But then, it'd be an 'efficient' failure. The profitability time-frame you set for your business will depend on some factors, including the nature of your industry, the market conditions and how much you're willing to invest in the venture. I have seen a lot of people dedicate their entire resources and years of hard work into failing enterprises. What's the point wasting ten years of your life working on a venture that has no scent of success? Although you validated the idea earlier on, it's still a business, and that means a risk. You should be flexible enough to ideas that don't seem to work for profitability.

6. Customer Acquisition

Before you get buried in the details of running a business, put together a customer acquisition plan. Think about how you get your first client, and how you get to your nth client. You may have the best business plan in the world, but without a customer you have no business. It's important that you create a thoughtful and strategic customer acquisition plan to guide your marketing and sales process right from day one. If you're looking for partners, investors or stakeholders, they'll also want to be convinced that you have a solid plan to get customers on board.

7.   Open Shop

At this stage, you have put everything you need together. It's time to open shop. A lot of entrepreneurs are tempted to wait until their product is 'perfect' so they can start selling. Have it in mind that 'perfect' is the contrary of good enough. As long as you don't have a product to present to your targeted prospects, you're flying blind. Part of implementing your business ideas is all about making a core product and getting it to market promptly. You can learn from your customers' reactions.

8.   Make Adjustments

You'll be getting a lot of feedback once your products hit the market. Use this feedback to make changes towards the betterment of your business or product. Also, monitor your marketing. If you're doing something wrong, you'll want to fix it. This is how companies improve and expand.

9.   Get Ready to Grow

Once your business gets going, you'll want to position yourself for growth. Revisit your business plan. Based on the feedback you have gathered, update your product, team, marketing and finance strategies. Just work on the things you didn't get right in the first place. Gather the resources you need to expand. If you want to raise capital to scale your business, do it. You should come up with a convincing pitch for investors.

10. Step on the Accelerator

When you have a market proved plan and the right resources in place, you are ready to expand. A business that is already successful the first few months or year has the potential for rapid growth. Make sure your team knows about your growth strategy and where you are heading. Your employees should be aware of your goals or objectives. This helps make implementation easier. Everyone should know what's expected of them.

6 TIPS FOR IMPLEMENTING NEW IDEAS IN YOUR BUSINESS

The steps highlighted in the previous chapter will help you implement your idea, but you'll need your best to make this implementation successful. This chapter presents some proved implementation tips and strategies that you can leverage. Proper execution of your brilliant business ideas is what makes the whole endeavor a success. To strengthen the new business, the management should spend enough time analyzing the various implementation options available.

1.   Get Staff Involved

New companies can start with any number of staff. If you want all your team members to accept your application and growth strategy, you'll need to involve them in the planning. This doesn't mean that you have to take input from each and everyone, especially if it's a large organization. Get your management level staff involved right from day one. If you're looking to make significant changes in the way things are done in the business, make sure to bring them on board beforehand. Everyone needs to feel that they are at the center and not on the sidelines of growth in the company.

2.   Train your Employees

At first, you can start with a small team of qualified individuals. But through the implementation process, you'll need to invest in your employees through training. Indeed, training should be done at the earliest convenience. For instance, if you're looking to implement a new idea, consider doing training 60 days prior. Focus on informing your staff about pending changes, and then explain how these changes will be beneficial for the enterprise. Carry on with training throughout the implementation phase, and be receptive to feedback from your staff regarding how the entire process could be made smoother.

3. Count in Outside Factors

Whenever you're looking to bring in a new idea to an existing business, think about how this could affect your relationship with vendors and customers. The parties you do business with are an important part of your enterprise. Discuss your new idea with your clients and suppliers to see whether you'll need to make any alternations in your plan.

4. Open Communication

Communication is key in any business. Implementing a business idea is easier if you encourage your employees to add their input and maintain an open communication policy throughout the implementation process.

5. Competencies

How you present your company or product has a great impact on whether or not it turns out a success. Here are five essential skills that separate dreamers from change-makers:

- *Packaging* – this is all about whether you're able to take your ideas and transform them into something you can sell. You need to be able to create a particular product that you can offer to the marketplace. At this stage, you already have scored on this competency.

- *Positioning* – are you able to align your offer to a strong market need? It's easier to build a business on demand than create an order around your products. Healthy companies can position themselves as a solution to a considerable problem in the market.

- *Influence* – are you able to influence buyers? This starts by convincing them that they need this product or service and then persuading them to part with valuable time, money or energy to get it from you.

- *Acceleration* – once you have done the hard work of presenting your product on the market, you need to get the most out of the opportunity you have created. As long as you're increasing demand for the product or service you offer, you'll be set on a path to growth.

- *Reinvention* – are you able to leverage your brand and expertise to open up new and bigger opportunities? Apple created the iPod and used it to capture the recorded music market.

6.   Build your Market

You need market building skills to take your idea to the next level after implementation:

- *Offer it* – sometimes, you don't know you need a product until you see one. Think about the first time you saw a flat screen TV, you probably didn't know you needed one.

- *Force it* – Apple used its massive customer base to become the dominant retailer in the recorded music industry.

- *Seed it* – find great ways to leapfrog your new product into the public eye. For an example, you may want to target celebrities.

- *Name it* – coin a new phrase to define the problem you are solving. For example, McKinsey & Co. used the label *"The War for Talent"* in the 1990s. This positioned them as a thought leader and the go-to HR consultancy firm.

- ***Spread it*** – create stories about your product. These stories should be highly emotive, and should be related to the market need you discovered with your idea.

Of course, every product or market is different. You'll need more perspiration than inspiration to implement your business ideas. But these tips will guide you to make sure that your best ideas finish last as great companies.

SUMMARY

At this stage, you know everything you need to come up with great business ideas and implement them. Today, hundreds of thousands of people are considering starting a home based business, and for good reasons. Regardless of the nature of the company you'd like to venture into, it often narrows down to the original idea. If the original idea isn't good enough or isn't market-proved, there's a high probability the resulting enterprise will fail within its two years! The knowledge you've gathered through this book is everything you need to make sure you do not invest your hard-earned cash in a failure-bound business idea.

You have the power to generate as many ideas as you can on a daily basis. By leveraging design thinking, you can refine your idea and set the stage for a successful business. The implementation tips you've learned in the later sections of this book are crucial to establishing a successful enterprise. The important thing is to start immediately. Don't just sleep on it. If you aspire to be a successful entrepreneur, identify at least ten business ideas daily. Within a week, you'll have over 60 options to choose from. Verification is also a critical step. Pay keen attention to verification. You have got everything you need in this book. Take action now!

ABOUT THE AUTHOR

Brad Jones is an internet marketer and digital entrepreneur. He now makes a 6 figure income by working online for myself running multiple businesses.

He started experimenting with earning money online back in 2002 on the side, whilst he continued working his 9-5 sales job. It wasn't until 2008 that he finally got to the point where his side income covered his monthly expenses, and he saw the opportunity to earn a lot more. He quit his job later that year and has been working for himself ever since.

Brads believes there are many people claiming how to make money online, and in his experience there is no ONE best way. He's found success in many avenues, and believes it's down to the individual's passions and interests that will produce the best results for them.

Brad has written several books demonstrating some of the ways you can make a living working online, and he's have found success in all of them.

"Be open to try new things, never quit, and you'll find the success you're looking for. I promise you!"

MORE BOOKS BY BRAD JONES

Blogging Brilliance – How to A Make Bundle on Your Blog

Ebay Excellence – Making Easy Money the Ebay Way

Fiverr Freedom – From Your First Gig to Making A Fortune On Fiverr

Flawless Freelance Writing – How to Make A Fortune Freelance

Storytelling – A Storytelling System to Deliver Inspiring and Unforgettable Speeches

You're The Problem – 30 Real Life Solutions to Stop Destructive Actions and Get Out of Your Own Way

Social Media – The Ultimate Guide to Transforming Your Brand with Social Media

www.ingramcontent.com/pod-product-compliance
Lightning Source LLC
Chambersburg PA
CBHW071012180526
45168CB00003B/1394